W9-BHG-508

FASCINATING FACTS

DOGS

BY MARIE PEARSON

The Child's World®
childsworld.com

Published by The Child's World®
1980 Lookout Drive • Mankato, MN 56003-1705
800-599-READ • www.childsworld.com

Photographs ©: Shutterstock Images, cover
(pharaoh hound), 1 (pharaoh hound), 2, 4, 7, 12,
13, 15, 17, 19, 20; Eric Isselee/Shutterstock Images,
cover (Bernese mountain dog), cover (Chihuahua),
1 (Bernese mountain dog), 1 (Chihuahua) 5,
10, 14, 18, 24, back cover (Dalmatian); Africa
Studio/Shutterstock Images, cover (Labrador
retriever), 1 (Labrador retriever), 9; Erik Lam/
Shutterstock Images, cover (basset hound), 1
(basset hound), 11; Erik Lam/iStockphoto, 6, back
cover (mastiff); Richard Peterson/Shutterstock
Images, 8; Borina Olga/Shutterstock Images,
16; Tania Volobueva/Shutterstock Images, 21

ISBN 9781503844629 (Reinforced Library Binding)
ISBN 9781503846227 (Portable Document Format)
ISBN 9781503847415 (Online Multi-user eBook)
LCCN 2019957693

Printed in the United States of America

ABOUT THE AUTHOR

Marie Pearson is a children's book editor and author. She has been obsessed with dogs since she was young and later worked as a dog groomer. She competes with her Australian shepherd and standard poodle in a variety of dog sports, and she still loves learning new facts about dogs.

CONTENTS

People have **bred** dogs for certain traits. Many of these traits make dogs good for special jobs. Dogs can pull sleds across the Arctic. They can protect and move large herds of livestock. They have fought in wars. They have helped people hunt for food.

4

◄ **Humans have lived with dogs for more than 15,000 years. Dogs were domesticated from a type of ancient wolf. Gray wolves also evolved from these ancient wolves. Since then, dogs have helped humans in many ways.**

Dogs can act and look different from each other. Some dogs like to chase small animals. Others are gentle with them. Some dogs are huge. Others are tiny. Dogs are the most physically **diverse** animals on Earth.

There are many amazing things to learn about dogs! ▶

CHAPTER ONE

A Dog's Body

The highest a dog has jumped is 6 feet (2 m). A greyhound named Feather set this record in 2017.

6

The largest litter of ▶ puppies a dog has had is 24. A Neapolitan mastiff named Tia gave birth to the huge litter in 2004.

Many dogs kick their feet into the ground after depositing waste to mark their territory. Dogs have scent **glands** in their feet. These glands give off a smell that tells other dogs who was there.

Circling before lying down is probably a habit dogs kept from their wild **ancestors**. The action in the wild would pat down snow and grass to make a bed. ▼

Senses

Dogs see in color. They just do not see as many colors as humans do. Dogs can see blues, greens, and yellows. Dogs also see better than humans at night. Their eyes reflect light in front of them like a flashlight.

A dog can smell .5 teaspoon of sugar mixed into an Olympic swimming pool. A dog's nose has as many as 300 million scent receptors. Humans only have six million. And relative to body size, the part of a dog's brain dedicated to scent is 40 times larger than that of a human's.

Puppies are born with their eyes and ears tightly closed. They start to see and hear at about two weeks old. ▼

Dogs only have 1,700 taste buds. Humans have up to 9,000.

Dogs can hear sounds people cannot. In addition to hearing what people hear, dogs can also hear higher-pitched noises.

Dogs use their sense of smell to ▶ help them taste food. Without their sense of smell, a dog could not taste the difference between chicken, fish, or beef.

Amazing Bodies

Every dog's noseprint is unique, like a human fingerprint. No other dog has a matching print.

Dogs can only sweat through their paw pads. The main way dogs stay cool is by panting. The dog breathes out warm air. This causes the saliva in its mouth to **evaporate**, helping the dog cool down.

◄ Floppy ears, spotted fur, and curly tails are linked to domestication. Russian scientists bred friendly wild foxes with each other. As each generation became tamer, traits such as spotted fur and floppy ears popped up.

Dogs have three eyelids. Like a human, they have a top and bottom lid. They also have a third eyelid in the inner corner of both eyes. This eyelid wipes dust and other things off the eye. The third eyelid also makes some tears to keep the eye healthy.

A dog's wet nose helps ▶ catch scents. The nose produces a **mucus** that keeps it wet. Smells stick to wet things better than to dry things. Wet noses also help dogs keep cool.

CHAPTER TWO

Living with People

38%

In the United States, 38 percent of households own dogs. There are 76.8 million pet dogs.

U.S. dog owners spend approximately $1,300 or more on each of their dogs every year. Dog expenses include veterinary care, food, toys, and training.

Petting a dog can be healthy for both dogs and humans. Petting helps lower a human's blood pressure, protecting that person against heart disease. Calmly petting a dog in its favorite spots also helps the dog relax.

When humans stare into their own dogs' eyes, it causes both the humans and dogs to feel more bonded. The act releases a chemical called oxytocin into both the humans' and dogs' bodies. Oxytocin is linked to the feeling of a close bond with others.

Pharaoh hounds come from Egypt and have existed since 4,400 BC. Paintings of these hounds can be found on ancient ◄ Egyptian tombs.

13

Behavior

Dogs usually poop facing north or south. Researchers do not know why.

Some dogs naturally alert their owners to serious health issues. Their sense of smell and other senses let them notice changes that people cannot. Some dogs detect cancer, predict seizures, or warn people of low blood sugar, all before the human shows any symptoms.

A wagging tail reveals a dog's mood. ▶ A vibrating tail held high and stiff means the dog may be unfriendly. A wide, sweeping wag means the dog is probably friendly. A wag to the left can mean the dog is scared. Wagging to the right can mean the dog is happy.

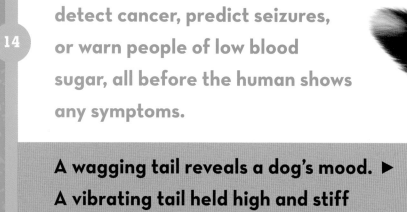

Barry the Saint Bernard saved more than 40 people in his life. Barry was born in 1800. He lived in the Alps mountain range on a pass between Switzerland and Italy. He found people who were lost or buried in the snow.

More than 300 dogs helped search for victims of the September 11, 2001, terrorist attacks in New York City. The dogs were specially trained to find people in the rubble. The attacks killed 2,753 people in New York. Other dogs helped comfort the people involved in the rescue work.

15

A Japanese Akita named Hachiko represents a dog's loyalty. Every day, Hachiko ▲ met his owner at the train station after work. One day, the Akita's owner died at work and did not come home. Hachiko returned to the station every day to wait for his owner until the dog died nine years later.

CHAPTER THREE

Breed Variety

Newfoundlands swim with a sort of breaststroke, not a doggie paddle. Their front feet push down and out. They also have webbed feet. These traits make them excellent water rescue dogs.

Rhodesian ridgebacks were bred ▶ to hunt lions in South Africa during the 1800s. A pack of ridgebacks would chase down a lion and keep the lion in place for the hunter. Many of these hounds have a ridge of fur down the spine.

A greyhound would beat a cheetah in a 1-mile (1.6-km) ▶ race. Greyhounds can run up to 45 miles per hour (72 km/h). They can reach that speed in just six strides. Greyhounds can also keep running 35 miles per hour (56 km/h) for up to 7 miles (11 km).

A Siberian husky could beat a greyhound in an **endurance** race. In the Iditarod sled race in Alaska, huskies travel almost 1,000 miles (1,609 km) over 14 days. That means they are pulling a sled 71 miles (114 km) per day.

Unique Features

Dalmatians are born white. Their spots come in as they get older. Weimaraners are born with stripes. Their stripes fade to a solid color a few days later.

A beagle's tail often has a white tip. This helped hunters spot the dog while hunting in tall grass.

The Norwegian Lundehund has six ▶ toes on each foot. These dogs were bred to hunt puffins in Norway. The extra toes helped the dogs climb steep, rocky land.

Basenjis do not bark, but they are not quiet. They make sounds similar to a yodel. This ancient breed has lived in central Africa for thousands of years. The first basenjis were not bred in the United States until the mid-1900s.

Samoyeds' lips curve up in a smile. This keeps their saliva from drooling and ▲ freezing on their faces. These dogs are from the cold northern region of Russia. They needed to stay warm in temperatures even colder than -60 degrees Fahrenheit (-51°C).

Breed Trivia

A border collie named Chaser learned the names of 1,022 objects, mostly toys. This earned her the description of world's smartest dog. Chaser died in 2019 at the age of 15.

The Dandie Dinmont terrier is the only dog breed named after a fictional character. It is named after a character in the 1814 novel *Guy Mannering* by Sir Walter Scott. The character Dandie Dinmont owns terriers. The breed comes in two colors: mustard and pepper.

Xoloitzcuintli is the official name for the ▶ breed commonly called the Mexican hairless. It is pronounced show-low-itz-kweent-lee, and owners often call it the Xolo. The Xolo can be mostly hairless or have a short coat.

The breed name poodle comes from a German word that means "puddle" or "to splash." Poodles are originally from Germany. They had many jobs, working as hunting dogs, herding dogs, army dogs, and more.

A Great Dane named Zeus holds the record for tallest dog. He stood 44 inches (112 cm) at the shoulder. The shortest dog is a Chihuahua named Milly. She is 3.8 inches (9.7 cm) tall at the shoulder.

An Alaskan malamute was filmmaker ▶ George Lucas's inspiration for the Star Wars character Chewbacca. Lucas owned a malamute named Indiana, who would stay close by when he wrote. So Lucas gave character Han Solo a furry companion.

Glossary

ancestors (AN-ses-turs) Ancestors are those from whom one has descended. Ancient wolves are the ancestors of dogs.

bred (BRED) When animals are bred, they are brought together to produce young. Humans have bred dogs with a variety of traits.

diverse (dy-VURSS) Something is diverse when there are many types that are very different from each other. Dogs are the most physically diverse animals on Earth.

domesticated (doh-MESS-tih-kay-ted) Something that has been domesticated has been made to live easily with humans. Dogs have been domesticated, but wolves have not.

endurance (en-DUR-ens) Endurance is the ability to keep going for long periods of time or thorough difficult tasks. Huskies are good at endurance races.

evaporate (ee-VAP-uh-rayt) To evaporate means to turn from water into water vapor. Warm air causes a dog's saliva to evaporate, cooling the dog.

evolved (ee-VOLVD) To have evolved is to have changed over time so as to better live in a certain environment. Gray wolves evolved from the same ancient wolves as dogs.

glands (GLANDZ) Glands are organs that release chemicals that the body can use. Dogs have scent glands in their feet.

mucus (MEW-kuss) Mucus is a slimy substance created by the bodies of animals. A dog's nose produces mucus.

receptors (ree-SEP-turs) Receptors are organs that receive specific molecules, such as scent molecules. A dog's nose can have 300 million scent receptors.

To Learn More

In the Library

Albee, Sarah. *Dog Days of History: The Incredible Story of Our Best Friends*. Washington DC: National Geographic Kids, 2018.

Miller, Mirella S. *Search and Rescue Dogs on the Job*. Mankato, MN: The Child's World, 2017.

Mills, Andrea. *The Everything Book of Dogs & Puppies*. New York, NY: DK Publishing, 2018.

On the Web

Visit our website for links about dogs:

childsworld.com/links

Note to Parents, Teachers, and Librarians: We routinely verify our Web links to make sure they are safe and active sites. So encourage your readers to check them out!

Index